PRACTICING
PEACE

GUIDEBOOK
31 Daily Meditations for Peace

PRACTICING
PEACE

GUIDEBOOK

31 Daily Meditations for Peace

Melinda Johnston

BUDDHI INSTITUTE

Embrace your Journey Within

Buddhi Press

Buddhi Press
500 Helendale
Suite 260
Rochester, NY 14609

Second Edition
Produced in the United States of America

Designed by Melinda Johnston
Edited by Teresa Schaeffer, Carrie Ladue and Ted Conley

Practicing Peace | Guidebook | 31 Daily Meditations for Peace

ISBN 978-0-9971410-0-9

This book is dedicated to all Peace Seekers.

CONTENTS

ADDITIONAL PRAYERS 88

ABOUT THE AUTHOR 93

ABOUT BUDDHI INSTITUTE 95

ABOUT BUDDHI PRESS 96

ACKNOWLEDGMENTS

This book is an inspired writing, and would not have come into being without the support of several people. Each of them holds an inner source of wisdom and foundational energy of light that has provided me with the motivation to prepare this guidebook, which offers 31 daily meditations for practicing peace.

Two very special women must be mentioned. In grace and gratitude, I honor Pat Crelly and Teresa Schaeffer, whose insight and companionship were essential forces in completing this book. Without their efforts, this book would not at all be possible.

With gratitude and a humble heart, I must next mention a group of women, the original Peacekeepers from our Authentic Women meditation group, for the launch of the *Season of Peace* 2015.

Being in the presence of their energy during our meditation sessions has continued to be an experience of perfect bliss, and awe. Thank you: Cindy (Buzz) Ansbrow, Sandy (Fahrvergnügen) Heerkens, Deborah (Smiley) Salber, Michelle (Congresswoman) Metallo, Rebecca (Slinky) Croucher, Nevada (Swiss) Ott, Dawn (Gigi) Teravainen, Lynn (Harvest) Stull, Lori (Muffin) Smith, and Cheryl (Super-hero) Coccia-Mock. The *Season of Peace* would not have "been" without you.

Also, thank you to the other Peacekeepers in the first *Season of Peace* who supported the cause, Cindy McDonald, Lisa Cashmere, Miriam Steinberg, Hong Nguyen, Janet Polk, Bette Landers, and the eternal Amy Weider.

Additionally, without the support and dedication from Lisa West, Kathy Kurz, Zahra Langford, Dr. Susan Schliff, Dr. Wendy Rosen, David Denz, Marge O'Keefe, and Tom Marsocci, the first edition of this book would have never been published.

I must also thank the inspirational Dr. Susan Tower Hollis. Thank you for our talks, your time, mentorship, friendship, and chocolate sharing. You challenged me to step up into finding the voice within.

And of course, my greatest source of inspiration for walking in peace, choosing peace, and practicing peace in equanimity, belongs to my ultimate hero, Mahatma Gandhi. The first time my eyes fell upon his quote, "Be the change you wish to see in the world," my heart sprang open, and clarity filled my mind with purpose. Such a simple quote, but from that day forward my life path had a new, and profound purpose.

Through Gandhi's *eyes* I could suddenly *see* that the purpose of life is to learn to love one another, and to treasure all creatures, great and small, through equanimity and compassion.

From this sudden insight, I was able to expand into a deeper understanding for practices in peace through the constant study of great spiritual masters such as Rumi, Mother Teresa, St. Francis of Assisi, and many others whose wisdoms are presented in this book.

I must also honor a few more of our world's Peacekeepers and their inspired actions, which illuminate all of us. Thank you to the Dalai Lama for believing that the world will be saved by the western woman. In humbleness, I pray that all of my actions are born within the intention for promoting peace, and that your shared dream may become realized through continued actions of all peoples.

Thank you to Pope Francis for again showing the world that kindness, compassion, and acceptance for all beings, is the greatest religion.

Thank you Thich Nhat Hanh. Your book, *Peace is Every Step* (1992) opened my eyes and heart many years ago. My favorite story from that book tells of the young woman who had temporarily put her smile inside a dandelion. Anyone who has ever walked me with knows that I am very mindful to not step on any dandelion, because a smile may be resting inside!

Thank you Dave Norton for teaching me "the Pause," and that everyone and everything is Pure, Perfect, and Complete. I do not know of a more simple wisdom than this, and it has forever changed my life.

Thank you Gita Ramachandran for showing me the seed packets of power contained inside of speech.

Thank you Cedric Grigg for teaching me how to *see* freedom in a new way, and also how to *hear* wisdom.

Thank you Stephanie Jablonoski Campanelli for leading that one yoga class, which allowed me to experience the present moment as the: Absolute Eternal All. That event of the self meeting the Self has forever changed my life.

And, of course, I must say thank you to Aimée Senise Conners for always sitting with me in the "chariot" during times of much needed deep contemplation.

Finally, thank you to all Practicing Peace readers. As more and more people engage in these practices, we become one body of consciousness in this steady process of cultivating peace for all beings.

INTRODUCTION

Practicing peace requires an unwavering, inward state of equanimity. We, as a collected group of peace seekers, must remain *seated* in peace, regardless of what's going on in the outside world. In equanimity, we allow all things to be what they are. No judging. No changing. We learn to allow all things, situations, and people to be fully expressed as what they are in that moment of time.

Mindfulness is the practice that teaches us to remain steady in both mind and emotion, so we may witness the Rational Mind's ideas of how things should be. Maintaining a state of inner peace, and accepting all conditions exactly as they are, requires a mindset of absolute love, faith, and compassion. Heart felt compassion is the necessary foundation for engaging oneself in inspired actions that carry a profound purpose.

This is a difficult task, but worth the reward. Learning how to practice peace in all environments and in all situations will expand your capacity for compassion. For example, any prayer you say for another is automatically a prayer for yourself. Through grace, the more you practice peace, the more peace will become you. Having perfect inner peace in all situations is the reward.

This guidebook also offers simple practices for those who may be trying meditation for the first time. However, this guidebook has been purposely written in a way to allow you, the reader, to enjoy your daily practice at any level of experience you are currently comfortable with.

When you are ready to share the inner peace you have cultivated, do so quietly. There is no need to tell others what you are doing, or to assert how anyone should practice peace, or how anyone should try to become more peace-minded. Your kind actions will speak for you, as you remain calm in all situations.

Keep in mind that there might be days in which you enter the world with your best intentions, yet still experience a challenging day. When this occurs, your meditation practice will be to seek refuge by going inward and once again cultivate inner peace for yourself. For days like those, this guidebook offers several techniques for re-acquainting yourself with your own inner space of personal refuge.

THIS BOOK'S PURPOSE

The first edition of this guidebook was prepared for the Authentic Women Meditation Group of Rochester, NY, and coincided with the *Season of Peace* global event organized by the Buddhi Institute. The *Season of Peace* is a 21-day, world-wide meditation event, designed to bring the people of the world together during December's holiday season.

The goal of the original event was to have people individually engage with the suggested peace meditation in this guidebook each day at 6 PM in their time zone. By doing so the world experienced meditative prayer, and peace contemplation for almost 24 hours a day from December 1, 2015 for the twenty-one days leading up to the winter solstice.

As the first *Season of Peace* began, many participants noticed that they were experiencing profound levels of inner peace, and wanted copies of the guidebook to give as gifts during the December holiday season. For this reason, the 2nd edition has been revised, and now offers 31 daily meditations for each day of the month.

The Practicing Peace Guidebook continues to be used by peace seekers around the world as increasing numbers of people engage with the daily meditations. *The Season of Peace* has expanded to become an on-going, year-long event as people engage with the prayers and mantras in this book day-by-day, each and every month.

May all of your actions be guided by the grace of peace, and may peace guide you and comfort you, always.

ABOUT MEDITATION

Meditation practice leads you to a sacred space within, and is established by allowing stillness of the mind to rise above your intellect. You will discover that in this *place* of introspection, perfect peace always exists. Through practice, the inward peace you cultivate during meditation becomes expressed outwardly in all that you do.

If you are just beginning your meditation practice, you may find the act of sitting in stillness to feel a bit awkward at first. This is normal.

A busy mind has difficulty settling, because it has had the freedom to hop around from thought to thought up until now. The ancient yogi sages refer to this as monkey mind, because similarly, the mind swings from thought to thought or sensation to sensation, while it attempts to make sense of incoming data from the five senses. Additionally, when the mind does not have something to focus on, it will create stories for the future, or re-examine experiences from the past.

Therefore, beginning meditation practice is simply a process of allowing the mind to do what it does, as you patiently witness the random thoughts coming and going, or rising and falling.

For this reason, it is important to not judge the thoughts while observing them. Do not become frustrated with them. The practice is to allow them to rise into our attention, and then fade away. Observing thoughts in this way is referred to as mindfulness or *awareness*.

Through concentrated awareness you remain focused on your breath, while the random thoughts come and go. The practices in this guidebook offer mantras, prayers, and visualizations to help you remain focused.

HOW TO PREPARE FOR EACH MEDITATION IN THIS GUIDE

Meditation practice allows you to realize a state of inner peace that is available in each and every present moment.

The practices offered in this guidebook are simple and easy to engage with. Some meditation guidebooks suggest that you buy certain candles and pillows, purchase CD's for guidance, use meditation benches…etc. I do not believe that purchasing such items is necessary for authentic meditation practice. But if this is your first attempt to practice meditation on your own; you may wish to create a sacred space in your home. Creating a routine for practice can be quite helpful as you begin meditation.

Realize that any level of meditation practice requires a commitment to oneself. There will be days in which you are very busy, or feeling tired, and you will not want to sit in meditation. Your mind may feel too scattered, or you may be influenced by an emotional disturbance, so a sense of overwhelm takes control of you. For these exact reasons, I encourage you to engage with your daily practice no matter what the conditions are of your mind or emotions. Noticing your mental and emotional fluctuations are actually part of the process, and allowing them to occur is fundamental to the practice.

On that note, the meditation practices in this guidebook purposefully teach you how to be-friend and then master the constant chatter of the mind. As you learn to become the witness to the inner dialogue, you will notice emotional blockages and old belief patterns fading away. Soon, you will become very comfortable sitting in your own reflection, and peace will begin to rise on its own.

To begin your Practicing Peace meditations for the next 31 days, the following suggestions are offered here:

1. CULTIVATE "SPACE"

Time: Give yourself about 15-30 minutes daily for your dedicated practice.

Distractions: Turn off the phone, TV, and put away anything that will distract you.

Get comfortable: A sitting position is recommended, because it allows you to remain alert. It is best if you can sit with a straight spine. A straight spine opens up the energy centers in your body, and allows the breath (prana) to revitalize you effortlessly.

If sitting for prolonged periods of time is difficult, you may choose a reclined position, or lying down. Please realize that if you are too comfortable, you may fall asleep. Meditation practice is very, very relaxing!

Ambiance: You may wish to dim the lights, or have a candle nearby. Create an environment so your mind will begin to anticipate the tranquil sessions that are about to follow. Ambiance sets the tone for going within.

2. ALLOW WHAT IS TO BE WHAT IT IS

Allowing: Some meditation practices will feel easy and peaceful. Other practices might pose more challenge as you attempt to settle the mind. Each session will feel different, and that is part of the practice! Meditation is a *container* of time in which no judgment of self needs to occur.

Emotions: Allow emotions to become your Teacher. If they arise, let them pass. Try not to avoid any emotion. As deeply engrained thought patterns begin to rise to the surface of the mind, you as the Observer, will notice that emotions are indeed entangled with thoughts.

Being the Observer of your mind, you witness the thoughts and emotions rising, and begin to see these fluctuations as *separate* from yourself. From a new level of understanding and perspective, you will experience the highest aspect of your mind, and become compassionate toward yourself as you learn to realize that the thoughts and emotions are occurring on their own.

You will notice through your own direct experience that inner peace and tranquility exist as one reality, and thoughts and emotions exist as a different *potential* reality. The calm witnessing of this phenomenon is called mindfulness, or awareness.

I encourage you to not push the thoughts and emotions away. Do not become troubled by them. Allow thoughts and emotions to rise and fall. Welcome them and thank them for being Teachers.

For example, perhaps during a sitting you notice a sensation of anxiety rising. This emotion may then produce an inner dialogue that prompts your mind to jump off track. Soon, you will notice that your mind has you thinking about other tasks you should be doing, or could be doing, instead of just sitting. When this occurs, allow the thoughts and emotions to pass. As the Observer, notice the fluctuation, and be patient with it. Then, gently guide your mind to come back into the practice, which may be a mantra, breathing meditation, or contemplative prayer.

Be kind to yourself. Hold peace and compassion for yourself as you experience fluctuations of the mind. They will pass.

Practicing Peace: By practicing peace in meditation, you will discover the simplicity of its presence.

However, if you have been experiencing a great deal of stress lately you may notice a whirlwind of emotions being stirred up in the beginning of your session. This is normal.

If peace has been absent from your life recently, coming inward, back into an authentic state of peace, may produce tears in the form of acceptance, joy, and re-remembering who you are. If this occurs, allow it to be. Thank yourself for coming back to peace.

In this place of re-discovery, you will have profound experiences while simultaneously sending peace to others during your daily meditation practices.

3. THE PRAYERS AND MANTRAS

The prayers and mantras offered in this book are suggestions derived from various spiritual philosophies and cultures.

If you have favorite spiritual texts or words of peace that comfort and empower you, then yes, by all means, bring those into your daily practice.

4. YOUR MEDITATION SESSIONS

There is really no wrong way to meditate. Trust your process. The vital path to inner clarity, and success, is to continue the practice.

As you learn to settle the constant chatter of the mind, and become the Observer, you will discover the subtle peace that belongs to the present moment. Inner peace, and the present moment are one and the same.

Through your continued practice, the rational mind begins to settle. The inner dialogue rests as inner peace rises. This state of inner peace cannot be obtained through intellect.

The present moment can only be experienced by becoming one with it. In other words, *to BE it*, or *to become It*.

The only way to BE in this infinite space of the present moment is to enter it *empty*. Empty means free of all hindrances, ideals, perceptions, thoughts, or beliefs.

Therefore, enter into your meditation practice empty and free of any expectation, goal or desire. Simply set an intention for cultivating peace, and allow the time spent in sitting on any day, to only be an experience of *that* sitting on *that* day.

As you prepare for each meditation practice, set an intention of becoming peaceful, of becoming peace minded, or of allowing peace to become you. Then do the practice. The practice will become your guide. The practice will carry you, and teach you along the way. Each of us has this inner wisdom within. Through practice you come into relationship with it.

I look forward to practicing peace with you, each and every day.

HOW TO USE THIS GUIDEBOOK

The purpose of this guidebook is to inspire people all over the world to meditate daily, and reflect on world peace by using the suggested mantra or meditation for each day's practice. By doing so, multitudes of people from around the world will be joined together as one, while we individually engage with the specific practice for each day of the month.

DAILY PRACTICE

Included in this guidebook are 31 days of quotes to reflect upon, a short teaching, and a suggested meditation practice, mantra, or prayer to contemplate.

I recommend reading the entire day's quote, teaching, and instruction prior to engaging with each day's practice. Allow yourself time to contemplate the teaching, and understand the type of meditation to be practiced for *that* day.

Each day's teaching asks you to "come into stillness." If you are just beginning your meditation practice, you may require a bit of time to actually settle the mind. Coming into stillness is the act of recognizing the present moment, and bringing your mind into a state of one-pointed concentration.

In my many years of practice, I have found the best way to enter the present moment is through an exercise called, **"The Pause."** This involves focusing the mind on only one of the body's senses at a time, allowing the *mind's eye* (The Observer) to fully witness: feeling, hearing, tasting, breathing, and finally seeing. By practicing The Pause, you train the mind to focus its attention on one *thing* at a time. The Pause narrows the mind's concentration to fully witness the body's senses one by one.

The instructions for experiencing The Pause are provided below. I suggest that you read through this entire practice so you will know how to guide yourself into fully witnessing the present moment. Some of my students have recorded the directions of this practice into their mobile phones, so they can listen to the directions step-by-step, while keeping their eyes closed.

THE PAUSE

* Sit comfortably. Be comfortable. Notice the position of your body. Notice how your feet feel on the floor. Notice how the shoes fit your feet. Become aware of how your pants feel on your body. Is the material soft or course? What is the temperature in the room? Do your hands and face feel warm, or is a cool breeze gently touching them? Notice the posture of your spine. Notice the weight and tension of your shoulders.

* Take in a deep breath. Hold at the top, and gently release the exhale. How does your breath feel exiting your nostrils? Is the movement of air soft and light, or rushed? Does the air feel warm as it passes your lip? Notice these things, and Be. Here. Now.

* Take pause. Sit. Be Still. Just breathe, and notice how your body feels experiencing the intake and exhalation of air. This is the present moment. This is you breathing. This is Now.

* Sit. Still. Here. Now…in this "space." Take notice of hearing. Let your hearing become wide. What sounds do you notice? Do you hear your breath? Is there soft rustling in the background? Do you hear cars or people outside? Is there music playing? Can you hear a clock? Just notice the sounds. Let the vibration of sound rise, and then fall. Notice all sounds, but try not to label them.

Be. Here. Now. Listen to the present moment. In this pause…Sit. Allow. Allow all tasks of the day to fade away. The only reality is you being here now.

* Notice taste. How does your mouth feel? Is there a feeling of warmth? Dryness? Perhaps you still experience a sweetness left over from your last meal. Swallow. Notice the sensations involved with this experience. No judging. Only noticing. Become aware of the heat, texture, elements in the present moment that involve taste. This is the present moment. Nothing more. Nothing less. It. Just. Is.

* Breathe. Feel the air coming into your lungs. Does your stomach rise and fall with each breath?? This is life. This is you breathing. This is now.

* Open your eyes. Take in the sensation of sight. See as you have never seen before. Take in color. Light. Texture. Depth. Perspective. Reflections. This is sight. This is seeing. Be. Here. Now, and see.

* Close your eyes. Feel your breath. Feel your body….notice its posture. Notice if you feel warm or chilled. Notice the floor meeting your feet. Breathe. Breathe again.

* You are Here. You are in this moment. This moment is Now.

You may now end the exercise. You have fully witnessed the present moment.

SOURCES OF INSPIRATION

Throughout your involvement with this practice, you may find that one simple mantra or prayer will bring you into an immediate place of peace. If this occurs, memorize it, or write it down and carry it with you.

As you begin to settle in for your daily practice, enjoy the simplicity of just sitting. Then as you focus on breath, you may begin to send love, peace, and joy to:

* *People that you know need peace and comfort.*

* *Groups of people, who are ill, in hospitals, or are homeless, scared...etc.*

* *The entire world of peoples, creatures and nature...etc.*

Your daily practice is your prayer offering--your intention, and your act of cultivating and sending peace.

May you have the courage to be a source of inspiration to others. May you have the ability to smile always. May you have a kind word to offer when others are hanging onto hope. May you have the ability to love all as One.

May the light in you, ignite the light in others.

~ DAY 1 ~

"Peace begins with a smile."

~ Mother Teresa

Peace begins within. In this first practice, we learn how to purposefully manifest joy within our own hearts, and then offer it as a gift to others.

Cultivating your own experience of inner joy is easy to establish when you settle the mind, and focus your attention inside of Heart Center.

Inside this higher level of awareness, you will personally come to know the existence of a calm and steady *peace* that is abundantly available inside each and every present moment.

Within full awareness of Heart Center, you become a vessel of joy, and are able to mindfully send this presence of peace outwardly to whomever you believe needs it the most.

SIMPLE HEART MEDITATION

Come into a comfortable sitting or reclined position. Close your eyes and allow stillness to occur. Focus on observing your inhale and exhale for 5 full breath cycles.

Now, bring your mind's focus to your Heart Center.

With each inhale, allow your awareness of Heart Center to expand. Guide your mind's attention to fully witness any sensation that this space in your body is experiencing.

You may need to remember a past time in which you were truly joyful. Relive such an experience in your mind, and allow the sensation of joy fill your own heart. Take as long as you need to breathe in joy.

Now, begin to imagine the joy you are experiencing to expand from Heart Center as a color or light.

As you experience your own inner joy, send its presence outward to a family member, friend, or group of people.   If idle thoughts begin to pop up into your mind, settle them with a mantra such as:

MANTRA

"May all beings be filled with Joy and Peace."

Allow each inhale to expand Heart Center with joy, and then sense the joy flowing out from you into the world. Try to maintain this for 10-15 minutes, or as long as you can.

When you are ready to end your practice, imagine light coming back to your Heart Center, and slowly open your eyes.

Sit for as long as you wish, and find comfort in the sense of joy and peace you have cultivated within.

"Lord, make me an instrument of thy Peace."

~ St. Francis of Assisi

This is the first sentence of one of my most favorite prayers. Using this simple, single sentence as a meditative mantra will establish you in the exact peace that it prays for.

When used repeatedly this mantra becomes a personified, vibrating, *"blanket of peace."* It becomes you, and radiates through you. You and the prayer become One.

MEDITATIVE PRAYER

The blessing of this prayer will affect you as much as those you might be praying for.

First, learn the **mantra.**

> "Lord, make me an instrument of thy Peace."

Next, close your eyes, and come to stillness. Focus on your breath for 5 full cycles of inhaling and exhaling.

Begin reciting the mantra in your mind slowly so you are able to FEEL the meaning of each word. Allow yourself time to experience the full intention of the mantra.

If you are new to meditation, your mind may become bored after just a few repetitions. If so, then stay with the meditation as long as you can.

Whenever you choose, come back into full Awareness, and read the rest of the prayer slowly to yourself. This is quite a powerful experience when you allow yourself to feel EACH word as you read it.

Or, you may choose a favorite line, and continuously recite that one. Repetitive prayer surrenders ego into a realm of higher consciousness.

THE FULL PRAYER

Lord, make me an instrument of thy peace.
Where there is hatred, let me sow love;
Where there is injury, pardon;
Where there is doubt, faith;
Where there is despair, hope;
Where there is darkness, light;
Where there is sadness, joy.

O divine One, grant that I may not so much seek...
To be consoled as to console,
To be understood as to understand,
To be loved as to love,
For it is in giving that we receive,
It is in pardoning that we are pardoned,
It is in dying to self that we are born into eternal life.

"An eye for an eye only makes
the entire world blind."

~ Mahatma Gandhi

Gandhi fully understood the Laws of the Universe, and
for this reason he knew that acts of violence would
only breed more violence.

When others condemn us, or display some other form
of un-kindness, it makes logical sense to protect
oneself. The most difficult practice is that of
equanimity, or maintaining a state of peace, no matter
what the outside world brings our way.

This practice requires us to re-visit each of our inner
beliefs and surrender those beliefs to our state of unwavering inner peace. Attaining and maintaining a
state of equanimity requires a life-long commitment to
its practice. You will be introduced to it in today's
meditation.

Let us begin by allowing peace to arise fully within.

BREATHING MANTRA MEDITATION

Come into a comfortable sitting or reclined position.

Close your eyes and allow stillness to occur. Focus on observing your inhale and exhale for 5 full breath cycles.

As you obtain stillness and are comfortable with it, begin the breath mantra meditation below.

INHALE MANTRA

"I breathe in Peace."

Imagine peace filling you with each breath you take.

EXHALE MANTRA

"I exhale Peace to All."

Imagine peace exiting your nostrils, and beginning to spread out into the world. Allow your Mind's Eye to guide you as you offer this gift to all peoples, and all beings.

Try to maintain this breathing mantra meditation for at least 10-15 minutes.

If it helps, you may wish to enjoy reading some inspirational texts just before and just after your meditation practice.

~ Om Shanti
(Perfect Peace)

~ DAY 4 ~

"For a day, just for one day, talk about that which disturbs no one and bring some peace into your beautiful eyes."

~ Hafiz

From: *The Subject Tonight is Love: 60 Wild and Sweet Poems* (2003)

Practicing peace requires a deep commitment. Today we will practice peaceful speech. Complaining, gossiping, or speaking about fears or worries are actions that are *not* rooted in peace.

For today, the practice is to become mindful of the words you speak for 24 hours. Only speak in kindness. Allow yourself to witness any thought that is not peaceful to rise into your awareness, yet refrain from speaking the words that would express those thoughts. Just notice them, and let them fade away on their own. Then, try to bring kindness to the forefront of your mind.

To help with today's practice, I recommend using the Buddha's Loving-Kindness prayer for this meditation session. The prayer is also quite comforting whenever you feel troubled by any thought or emotion.

LOVING-KINDNESS MEDITATION

During this meditation, focus on each sentence one at a time, and recite the mantra to yourself while also FEELING the emotion of each word. Feeling each word *is* the practice.

Recite the entire 4 lines of the stanza to yourself, and repeat each stanza at least 3 times.

THE PRAYER MANTRA
Begin with this stanza for 3 repetitions:

> May all beings have peace.
> May all beings live with ease.
> May all beings be happy.
> May all beings have love.

Now, think of people you know that you have recently felt ill will toward.   Recite the mantra below 3 times while thinking of them.

> May (this person) have peace.
> May (this person) live with ease.
> May (this person) be happy.
> May (this person) have love.

Please continue this mantra for every person, types of people, or groups of people you have ever had difficulty with.

If you can, recite the mantra 3 times for each person that comes to mind, and 3 times each for every group of people that normally disturb you.

If you notice any change of emotion occurring, allow the emotion. Peace is overcoming deeply buried belief patterns belonging to the subconscious mind.

When you are ready, you may end the meditation. I generally try to stay with the full mantra practice for at least 20 minutes.

"World peace must develop from inner peace. Peace is not just mere absence of violence. Peace is, I think, the manifestation of human compassion."

~ Dalia Lama XIV

Inner peace blossoms as we learn to offer compassion toward ourselves. This is part of the spiritual growth process. As self-compassion expands, you become able to see all other beings with a new level of expanded compassion.

The gift of self-compassion awards you with the ability to *not* take anything personally. You come to realize that each person has their own struggles and obstacles to overcome in their own lives.

In light of this realization, you experience the peace and inner freedom that compassion contains. You come to realize that compassion allows you the ability to help and offer kindness to others easily, with no attachment to the outcome. You do not expect reward, praise, or returned kindness. At this level, compassion is quite similar to unconditional love; therefore, you need nothing in return. You love for love's sake, and nothing else.

But, to experience such inner peace and freedom, you must first offer yourself complete self-acceptance.

COMPASSION MEDITATION AND MANTRA

Come into a comfortable sitting or reclined position. Close your eyes and allow stillness to occur. Focus on observing your inhale and exhale for 5 full breath cycles.

As your breath rises and falls, focus on Heart Center. Notice it. Offer your heart absolute unconditional love. See your heart space as radiant and glowing.

Maintain this focus for at least 5 minutes. If your mind begins to wander, gently bring it back with the reminder, **"I am perfect Love."**

MANTRA

After you have filled your Heart Center with unconditional love, you may now begin to send it outward to anyone or everyone.

You will notice a more vibrant shift if you allow yourself to FEEL each word as you slowly recite it within your mind.

"May all Beings know this Love."

"May all Beings share this Love."

"May all Beings accept this Love."

"May all Beings become this Love."

Try to stay in the mantra for 10-15 minutes before coming back into full waking consciousness. Enjoy a heightened presence of extraordinary peace and comfort after completing this meditation.

"The first peace, which is the most
important, is that which comes
within the souls of people when they
realize their relationship, their oneness
with the universe and all its powers,
and when they realize at the center
of the universe dwells the Great Spirit, and
that its center is really everywhere,
it is within each of us."

~ Black Elk

Another way to practice peace is to acknowledge that each of us, (the animal kingdom included) is a unique expression of life created by one Source.   Each of us is an amazing expression of the one Divine Creator.

Often we can appreciate this concept, but to fully know it, to fully experience the one Source existing within all beings, we must leave behind the logic belonging to our five senses. We must rise into a level of consciousness that fully realizes the nature of *all* things.

Today's contemplative meditation prayer asks for inner guidance as we practice honoring the *sacred essence* existing within all created beings.

Read the prayer, and contemplate the meaning of the words. Allow yourself to FEEL the words as you read them.

NATIVE AMERICAN PRAYER FOR PEACE

O Great Spirit of all living things, I raise my heart, my mind, and my soul to you. May the messengers the four winds hear this prayer.

By flight of the winged eagle kingdom may this prayer be brought to you. Mother Earth who cares for your creations, may we receive your Blessing.

May we see each part of creation as an expression of your Divine Presence.

O Great Spirit, give us the wisdom to teach ourselves and our children to love, to respect, and to be kind to each other, so that they may grow with peace in mind.

May we learn to share all the good things you provide for us on this Earth. May we see your face in the diversity of all of your magnificent Creation.

~ Mitakuye Oyasin **"All my Relations"**

"The mind can go in a thousand
directions, but on this
beautiful path, I walk in peace.
With each step, the wind blows. With
each step, a flower blooms."

~ Thich Nhat Hanh

Thich Nhat Hanh is a famous Vietnamese Buddhist monk, who authored one of my favorite books; Peace is Every Step (1992). The book focuses on mindfulness practices, but the teachings reveal that by maintaining present moment awareness, each of us can easily achieve inward peace, and then radiate outward from that place of peace.

In this way, we become the change we wish to see in the world, step-by-step, moment by moment.

THE TEACHING

May grace be our guide as we practice peace. Many times we become distracted and then fall victim to our mind as it runs off with worry or concerns when Ego grasps toward experiences with the desire to gain happiness. By grasping for happiness, we step out of peace.

The best way to come back into authentic joy is to forget your troubles, and instead pray or meditate for the well-being of others. Anytime you notice your mind contemplating worries or concerns, try this prayer.

A PEACE PRAYER

May all beings who are limited with sufferings of body and mind, now be freed from their illnesses.

May those who are frightened cease to be afraid, and may those bound or oppressed by others now become free.

May the weak and powerless now find power.

May people full of fear and hate, now begin to cultivate kindness toward each other.

May those who are lost inside of addiction and other harmful habits, now find wholeness in heart, body and mind.

May those with no voice now become heard.

May Love now protect and guide all beings.

~ Om

"Returning violence for violence multiplies violence, adding deeper darkness to a night already devoid of stars... Hate cannot drive out hate: only love can do that."

~ Martin Luther King Jr.

Martin Luther King Jr, was a beautiful Peacekeeper. He had a dream that continues to shine through the hearts of many, now yourself included.

Today's meditation practice will have us send forward the dream of peace, so that this dream may enter the minds of those who are either afraid to have this dream, or have been struggling for so long--perhaps they have forgotten how to dream at all.

Our dream is for all to know peace, want peace, and live for peace. The practice today is creative visualization as meditation.

A DREAM OF PEACE MEDITATION

Come into a comfortable sitting or reclined position. Close your eyes and allow stillness to occur.

Focus on observing your inhale and exhale for 5 full breath cycles and begin to cultivate a state of peace within. Invite peace to become you.

To do this, you may use a mantra such as:

"I am absolute Peace,"

Or with each inhale state to yourself,

"I now breathe in Peace."

Imagine the peace you have cultivated to become like a bright shimmering cloud of glitter, or light, that rises into the night sky.

Imagine each inhale expanding the size of this shimmering cloud. See it glittering as "particles of intention." Your cloud is packed with the intention of inner peace for all.

Use breath to expand the intention, and the exhale to *move* the cloud. Move the cloud to the part of the world that is now sleeping in the night hours.

Allow your mind's eye to see your cloud of intention float down from the sky into individual homes...landing on the forehead of any person currently sleeping. May they dream of peace! See your "intention" of peace touch them gently, so that the idea of peace may enter them, guide them, and protect them.

See this happening now. "See" peace entering the minds of all who are now sleeping. Sit with this visualization for as long as you can.

~ May you Be this Peace

"If peace is really what you want, then you will choose peace."

~ Ekhart Tolle

Ekhart Tolle is a modern day master who teaches mindfulness practices, and how to live fully from within the present moment.

As we learn to calm the constant chatter of the mind, the inner dialogue and its fears, we begin to realize that inner peace is a constant state of reality that exists within each of us. It is an unwavering presence. Yoga masters refer to this state of being as, Sat Chit Ananda, which means, *True Consciousness* is *Bliss*.

Once realized, we come to know that in each present moment we are offered a choice of what to believe in. We may choose to establish ourselves within this presence of constant unwavering peace, or we may choose to experience the "whirlpool" of thoughts belonging to an untrained mind. The latter, steers us into beliefs that we must fix something, gain something, conquer something, and acquire something. In this mindset, we suffer from lack of peace while attempting to obtain the peace we are seeking.

Peace is always a choice, from moment to moment. A calm mind knows this. In today's practice, we learn to cultivate all that the present moment offers.

SIMPLICITY AND PEACE IN THIS MOMENT

Come into a comfortable sitting or reclined position.

Close your eyes and allow stillness to occur. Focus on observing your inhale and exhale. Do this for 5 full breath cycles.

Now, bring your attention to your mind's eye. This is the space in-between your eyebrows.

Sense this space either right on your forehead, or a couple of inches in front of your forehead. Imagine that your real eyes can see this "point" of the mind's eye about 3 to 8 inches in front of the eyebrows.

You may wish to give this *point in space* a color, or a color may appear on its own as you narrow your concentration to this point in space.

Use each inhale to increase whatever your mind's eye presents to you, and use each exhale to maintain it.

Realize that you may "see" nothing, and instead simply notice a sensation in that place.

Allow yourself to become fully established as the Observer, and focus all of your concentration at this space between the eyebrows.

If you notice your mind wandering off, bring it back with a mantra such as:

"I am now in the Peace of this present moment."

The goal of the practice is to maintain one-pointed peaceful awareness for as long as you can.

When you are ready, come back into full awareness and thank yourself for enjoying the present moment.

"May you be at peace,
May your heart remain open.
May you awaken to the light of your own
true nature. May you be healed,
May you be a source of healing
for all beings."

~ Tibetan Buddhist Prayer

There is real power in the repetition of a mantra as a form of meditation. The practice of repetition works very much like an invisible "corkscrew." As the mantra burrows in, it releases all old belief patterns that oppose it, while also quieting the mind, allowing for longer meditation sessions.

For this reason, mantra meditations offer the perfect refuge while attempting to cultivate stillness, since the mantra unlocks your greater virtues buried deep within.

In recognition of this, Tibetan monks chant Om, or other sounds, allowing them to sit for hours in meditation with ease and comfort.

We only need to sit for 15- 30 minutes for our daily peace practices; nevertheless, if you often find your mind wandering while practicing meditation on your own, you may find using a mantra to be very helpful.

ABOUT THIS MANTRA

This is very similar to the Buddha's loving-kindness meditation, but the focus here is on you. Used on a regular basis, this mantra will effortlessly increase your capacity to be at peace. Your heart will become open and unafraid, allowing you to come into an awareness of your highest nature, so that YOU may be a source of well being for all others.

THE PRACTICE

As you say each word in your mind, FEEL the words. You will keep your eyes open during this practice, unless you are able to record or memorize the words below.

You may want to light a candle, and dim the lights. Take time and create space and really enjoy this. Allow the mantra to naturally lift you into a place of inner peace.

Recite each line slowly, and repeat the entire mantra 3 times.

May I be at peace,
May my heart remain open.
May I awaken to the light of my own true nature.
May I be healed.
May I be a source of healing for all beings.

Peace begins within you.

~ **Om shanti**

"Do everything with a mind that lets go. Do not expect any praise or reward. If you let go a little, you will have a little peace. If you let go a lot, you will have a lot of peace. If you let go completely, you will know complete peace and freedom. Your struggles with the world will have come to an end."

~ Achaan Chah

"Letting go" is another practice in peace, that when understood and applied, you obtain an unwavering and unshakable state of inner peace and calm. The idea of letting go can be unsettling for some, because to the rational mind, *letting go* feels like we are losing something, or giving part of ourselves away.

I can assure you that nothing is lost, but all is gained.

Consciously choosing to let go allows the Rational Mind to release fear. Love comes rushing in, and you acquire the gift of being able to "see" from your Heart Center.

In the absence of fear, you now experience having compassion and understanding for all beings. Peace begins to move you through life with a quiet confidence, and free spirit.

THE MEDITATION

Come into a comfortable sitting or reclined position. Close your eyes and allow stillness to occur.

Focus on observing your inhale and exhale for 5 full breath cycles.

Begin to smile as you continue to focus on breath.

Now, imagine your smile lowering down into your Heart Center. Perhaps you can visualize your smile on an elevator, or a string that lowers down to the center of your chest.

Place your smile within your Heart.

Continue the meditation allowing each inhale to expand the sensation of love within your Heart Center. Allow yourself to fully experience pure, perfect, love. As you experience this heightened sense of love expanding within, make this statement:

"I release everything that is not this Love."

Imagine any old aches or fears flying out of your back, opposite of Heart Center. See your back opening like a door or a window, which allows everything that is not love to exit your body. This might take a while!

When your heart feels open and free, send out this prayer of intention:

"May All know and receive this Love."

When you are ready, you may end the meditation.

"But I say to you who hear, love
your enemies, do good to those who
hate you."

~ *Luke 6:27*

The act of loving all beings is the greatest practice among the
perennial philosophies. Here, in this famous passage in the
Gospel of Luke, the lesson is taught by Jesus of Nazareth.

It makes no rational sense to hold love in our hearts toward the
ones that hurt us or frighten us. This level of unwavering love
and compassion is recognized by most spiritual teachings to be
of utmost importance for enlightenment, and true peace of heart.

In prayer we ask for the presence of the one Source, as the
perfect Love existing within, to operate through us when we are
too weak or encumbered by pride, fear, doubt, and other
hindrances belonging to the rational mind. We pray for Love to
teach us how to love those we cannot.

PRAYING FOR YOUR ENEMIES

In this prayerful meditation practice, I ask you to go
beyond the boundaries of your rational mind, and sit in
peace as you pray for your enemies.

There will always be news headlines of murders, terrorist
events, horrible acts of violence, and political oppression.

As a result, the rational mind either finds a need to judge the actions of these events, or feel victimized by them.

To overcome this, one must consider that if one person suffers, we all suffer. Even the enemy that created the crime suffers. For this reason, and throughout millennia, spiritual teachers have instructed us to pray for enemies.

During this meditation, you may wish to first sit with some inspirational texts to settle your mind, and calm your heart. You may need to first pray that Love be allowed to love through you. Humble yourself, and become a vessel for perfect Love to flow through.

Then resolve to pray.

> *I pray for those that have done harm that they may find peace within.*
>
> *I pray that their families are unharmed, and are able to find peace.*
>
> *I pray for the ones in prison, that they may open their hearts in peace, that they may know love, and become whole through Absolute Love.*

Then, as you think of them...love them. Send them pure love, knowing that they too are children of God. May they know love, and become whole through the highest Love.

This practice is very healing for both you and them.

When you are settled, you may end the meditation, and allow peace to remain in your heart.

"Peace cannot be kept by force; it can only be achieved by understanding."

~ Albert Einstein

As our world continues to experience a growing increase in terrorist events and unimaginable acts of violence, each of us are left to process our own emotions from being the witness to such inexplicable actions.

When these events occur, news spreads quickly across multiple sources of media, which makes it easy for our old belief systems to come into play. From habitual patterns of the mind, we often seek someone to blame as the rational mind attempts to make sense of the situation.

When the rational mind is able to "fixate" on who to blame, it then knows who to avoid, or who to take revenge upon. It is this fight or flight mentality that allows one to believe that violence is best overcome with returned acts violence. Retaliation may temporally allow us to feel safe, however; taking this type of action separates us from each other at an increased degree, which only creates more suffering.

When violence or terror occurs, what the world needs at that time is compassion and understanding for *all* involved. Only then can the truth can come to light, and peace become known.

Today's practice again engages us in contemplative prayer.

For this prayer, allow yourself to come to stillness before reading the lines below. Go slowly, and become mindful of the meaning of each sentence. **I recommend sitting with each line of the prayer for 5 full breath cycles.**

A PRAYER FOR PEACE AND UNDERSTANDING

Lord, may I have eyes to see, and ears to hear.

When acts of violence and hatred occur, may I respond in acts of perfect love and understanding for all involved.

May any thoughts of judgment, revenge, or malice be removed from my heart and mind.

May my words comfort those in need of comfort.

May wisdom become me as a source of peace and clarity.

May forgiveness fill me, as I strive to understand the acts of those that cause pain and suffering to others.

I now pray for comfort to surround those in pain, who feel unheard, afraid, or separated from You.

I now pray that the heart and mind of every being always act from perfect peace, love, and understanding.

I pray that we learn to see You in the eyes of every soul we meet. May we all accept your peace and become that Peace.

MANTRA
Finish your practice today with the mantras below:

May I always offer Peace.

May I always offer Love.

May I always offer Understanding.

"It isn't enough to talk about peace.
One must believe in it. And it isn't
enough to believe in it
- one must work at it."

~ Eleanor Roosevelt

Many of us regularly contemplate peace, wish for peace, and step into service for others when it is for people that we know, and are comfortable with.

Working toward peace goes beyond seasons or certain holidays that recognize peace. Peacekeepers know that service to others, and kindness toward others, must be exercised daily.

Today's practice begins to expand your capacity for compassion. Through practice we learn how to expand our current level of compassion to also include people we previously have not felt comfortable with, or for persons whose point of view we may not understand.

Expanding our ability to offer compassion is cultivated by expanding our level of inner peace within.

INNER PEACE MEDITATION

Come into a comfortable sitting or reclined position. Close your eyes and allow stillness to occur. Focus on observing your inhale and exhale for 5 full breath cycles.

Become the Observer and just sit to witness your thoughts. Within moments, your mind will begin to wander since we are not using a focused prayer or mantra today.

Allow your thoughts to come and go. Allow them to pass by. Simply observe the contents of the mind, and observe any *emotion* that may rise with a particular thought.

Today, we fully accept, allow, and love ourselves, no matter what we witness and experience from the Inner Dialogue.

However, if you become "hooked" onto any thought that creates any sense of anxiety, or if a thought begins to take shape as a "story of the mind," say to yourself:

"I am not this thought. I am not this emotion."

"I now accept peace as the only possibility of this present moment."

Practicing this choice in meditation trains the mind to always choose peace in any given moment, and will assist you greatly in your day-to-day living.

Over time, this practice will allow you to offer patience and compassion to all people, no matter what their behavior is, or what they might be saying.

This practice trains the mind AND emotions to remain steady and peaceful, even when other people may attempt to disturb us with their words and actions.

This is how we work toward peace, no matter what.

"Out beyond ideas of wrongdoing
and rightdoing there is a field.
I'll meet you there."

~ Rumi

Rumi was a 13th century poet and mystic of the Sufi order. His deeply profound writings perfectly express the essence of peace, inner devotion, and a love for God. Each poem is composed of just a few short stanzas, yet they are brilliant, beautiful, and absolutely breathtaking.

The stanza above is one of my favorites. It acknowledges that there is a place in the heart and mind, a *field of knowing*, that accepts all conditions as they are. Love is the bridge between what our rational mind considers to be right or wrong, and a state of consciousness that is able to forgive all.

Agreeing to meet someone in this place means all is forgiven, and that perfect peace already exists, and has always existed.

This level of forgiveness requires a humble heart, so that Grace is the agent of the forgiving. This concept embodies all the practices we have learned over the past 14 days.

FIELD OF PEACE MEDITATION

Come into a comfortable sitting or reclined position. Close your eyes and allow stillness to occur.

Focus on Observing your inhale and exhale for 5 full breath cycles.

As you go deeper into stillness, begin to imagine in your mind's eye, a beautiful, peaceful field in nature. See this.

Allow your mind's eye to witness hearing birds or the wind, or a stream of water. Allow your mind's eye to smell the flowers or the breeze. Allow your inner and very creative mind's eye to really BE in this place.

See yourself sitting there, perhaps under a tree, and allow yourself to feel a sense of perfect contentment from being in this place. Imagine feeling unencumbered, unafraid, whole, and complete. You are at perfect ease.

AN INVITATION

Now, imagine someone that you have had great disdain for, or someone who has done you wrong, or who has caused you pain, to arrive in this field in front of you.

Allow them to come closer and closer, while you remain peaceful. Invite them to sit in front of you. As they do, see their body change into an incredible source of light.

Allow their vibration to change in and out of a variety of forms, until you "see" a form you are comfortable with.

Sit in this space with them. Just sit. No need for words. Just allow the *best* of each of you to be together.

When you are ready, end the mediation or invite others to come meet you in this field of peace.

This is a very healing meditation practice.

"Peace does not mean an absence of conflicts; differences will always be there. Peace means solving these differences through peaceful means; through dialogue, education, knowledge; and through humane ways."

~ Dalai Lama XIV

Today we deepen our practice. Through mindfulness, we have explored acceptance, allowing, and forgiveness. In the quote above, the Dalai Lama suggests that peace activism must be applied in all aspects of day-to-day living.

Purposefully engaging in mindful activism is a more difficult practice. It is quite easy to be established in peace while in meditation, and in the comfort of our homes or group meditation sessions.

When we are out participating in our day-to-day lives, conflicts do arise, from which old behavior patterns belonging to the subconscious mind easily explode to the surface of the rational mind. The subconscious mind generally produces an emotion, which then produces a thought, which then becomes an action.

We must carry the peace we have found through meditation with us in all that we do.

BUDDHIST PRAYER FOR PEACE

Come into a comfortable sitting or reclined position.

Close your eyes and allow stillness to occur. Focus on observing your inhale and exhale for 5 full breath cycles.

Invite peace to rise within.

Stay focused on your breath. Allow your Inner Dialogue to rise and fall. Allow all thoughts to be what they are. Just witness them in each present moment during this meditation.

If any disturbing thought or emotions comes, allow those as well, and then say to yourself,

"I invite peace to become my true Nature."

Sit with that statement, and repeat as necessary during this session.

When you are ready, you may end the session.

Please recite the prayer below after your meditation:

May my heart become full with compassion toward myself, and toward all living beings.

I now pray that all living beings realize that we are all brothers and sisters. May we all come to realize that we are all nourished from the same, one Source of life.

~ Om

"Restlessness and impatience
change nothing except our peace and
joy. Peace does not dwell in outward
things, but in the heart prepared to
wait trustfully and quietly on Him
who has all things
safely in His hands."

~ Elisabeth Elliot

In day to day living, conflicts or challenges need solutions. Most of us are busy, goal-oriented people who are willing to take any action necessary to solve a problem, complete a task, or achieve a goal.

Achieving goals becomes easier once we learn to invite inner peace to be part of the process. Stress melts away, and tasks are completed through a simple grace when we are aware of what our base intention is for any goal we have in mind.

Through meditation practice, we learn how to slow down our thoughts so we can witness the intention of each thought. We learn to "pause" before we speak, or before we act in our day-to-day living.

Learning to pause invites peace to be our guide, so we come to know the true intention of any desired action before we engage with that action. Contemplation assists us with inner awareness.

CONTEMPLATING SCRIPTURE
Matthew 6:25, 27, 31-34: 25

Inspirational texts are helpful when our mental habits again spin off into worry or concerns over day-to-day tasks.

In today's practice, I suggest reading the passages below, and then sit in contemplation. Allow yourself time to reflect on the meaning of the teachings.

"Therefore I tell you, do not worry about your life, what you will eat or drink; or about your body, what you will wear. Is not life more important than food, and the body more important than clothes?

Who of you by worrying can add a single hour to his life?

So do not worry, saying, 'What shall we eat?' or 'What shall we drink?' or 'What shall we wear?'

For the pagans run after all these things, and your heavenly Father knows that you need them.

But seek first his kingdom and his righteousness, and all these things will be given to you as well.

Therefore do not worry about tomorrow, for tomorrow will worry about itself. Each day has enough trouble of its own."

Always invite wisdom to become you prior to taking action.

~May this Peace become known, Amen

"Nonviolence is only for the brave men and women of the world because it requires courage – courage to love the beauty of life, beauty of humanity and the beauty of the world."

~ Amit Ray

From: *Nonviolence: The Transforming Power* (2012)

It takes absolute courage to trust the higher wisdom within, especially when we feel we are being provoked in the midst of conflict. Generally, our natural response is to protect our ideals and sense of rationale. However, striking back, physically or verbally, only brings more pain and suffering where pain and suffering are already present.

By remaining committed to only speak with kindness, and in a peaceful, calm manner, you invoke your higher wisdom. When you feel you are being provoked, you must learn to pause and allow your inner wisdom to "act for you, through you, and because of you."

However, holding our tongue is often viewed as cowardly. In society's standards, we are encouraged to stand up and fight! Winners are viewed as accomplished heroes.   Yet, the spiritual texts tell us to "kill with kindness," but to do so, requires releasing the Ego.

THE HEART SEES IN KINDNESS

In this meditation, we learn to "see" with the heart. When you can achieve this, you begin to experience a new reality, in which you recognize the Divine in all persons, all creatures, and all expressions of life. Being aware of the Divine nature of all things, any desire to cause harm to others fades away. You become incapable of causing harm to anyone, because such an idea can never enter the mind when living from Heart Center.

THE MEDITATION

Come into a comfortable sitting or reclined position. Close your eyes and allow stillness to occur. Focus on observing your inhale and exhale for 5 full breath cycles.

Now, begin to reflect back on your day and begin to recall the vast amounts of strangers you passed by. Think of the guy that cut you off in traffic. Think of the bank clerk, or check-out person at the store, or perhaps a neighbor. Think of these persons, and see them as they were, busy in their daily activity.

Now, in this creative visual meditative place of peace, imagine yourself hugging them. They can't see you; they don't know you are there.

It is from the mind's eye that you "see" yourself expand and become able to surround them with your presence. FEEL yourself engulf them with a hug. Hold them there in the space of your Heart Center, and let the love flow. Go back and hug everyone you had conflict with today, and anyone else you feel could use a little love.

You may end the session when you are ready.

"Ultimately, we have just one moral duty: to reclaim large areas of peace in ourselves, more and more peace, and to reflect it toward others. And the more peace there is in us, the more peace there will also be in our troubled world."

~ Etty Hillesum

Knowing when to take refuge for yourself is just as important as the act of maintaining peace in your day-to-day activities.

Over the course of history, great spiritual masters have recommended solitude as the one Source of peace for you to rely on.

For this reason, establishing a regular meditation practice for solitude is absolutely necessary for your well-being. You must rest, restore, and rejuvenate so you may continue to shine as a light in our world.

Be the peace that you seek.

BREATHING MANTRA MEDITATION

Today we re-visit the practice from day 3. Due to the simplicity of this practice, I recommend you engage with it on a regular basis.

Come into a comfortable sitting or reclined position.

Close your eyes and allow stillness to occur.

Focus on observing your inhale and exhale for 5 full breath cycles.

As you obtain stillness and are comfortable with it, begin the mantra meditation below:

INHALE MANTRA

"I breathe in Peace."

Imagine Peace filling you with each breath you take.

EXHALE MANTRA

"I exhale Peace to all."

Imagine peace exiting through your nostrils, and beginning to fill the world.

Try to maintain this breathing mantra meditation for at least 10-15 minutes.   If it helps, you may wish to enjoy reading some inspirational texts just before and just after your meditation practice.

~ Om Shanti

"But I have come to learn there is no peace while others suffer."

~ Lily Blake

From: *Snow White & the Huntsman* (2012)

This ideal is the foundational purpose of keeping peace, creating peace, and being established in peace.

If we believe that all things are created from one Source, then it must be true that each of us are also an expression of that one Source. If this is our foundational belief, then it must also true that each of us are part of one body of humanity. If one suffers, we all suffer.

Think about it. This is why it feels good when we take care of each other. As we do, we take care of ourselves. As we engage in random acts of kindness, we are essentially offering kindness to all beings. All things are connected.

The more you practice this, the more you will "see" that the ladybug and the snake are the same. The baby and the old person are the same. The people *here* are the same as the people over *there*.

We are all One.

KNOWING THE ESSENCE OF ONENESS

Come into a comfortable sitting or reclined position. Close your eyes and allow stillness to occur.

Focus on observing your inhale and exhale for 5 full breath cycles. As you obtain stillness, silently *declare* to yourself the mantra below with each inhale:

"I am That."

Imagine that your spirit is not only in you, but in all other people, and all living things.

"I am That."
Imagine that everybody is a reflection of yourself.

"I am That."
Imagine peace in your heart as the peace in every heart.

"I am That."
Imagine the fears in your mind as the fear in all minds.

"I am That."

Now surround yourself with a light that consumes any fear. Allow your mind's eye to feel everything that is not peaceful within you lifting up and leaving your body.

Imagine all beings feeling free and unafraid.

You may end today's session whenever you are ready.

~ Peace to All, always.

"The true and solid peace of nations consists not in equality of arms, but in mutual trust alone."

~ Pope John XXIII

The act of trusting others, and our own mind, is nurtured through the dedication of one's spiritual practice.

Absolute trust requires being detached from outcomes. Trusting also requires forgiveness of past misunderstandings, by realizing that any wrong actions we have ever engaged in, or any poor action from others, were only reflections of belief patterns based in fear, judgment, haste, oppression…

You cannot experience inner peace without first forgiving all actions from the past. This stands true even on a global scale. We must forgive ourselves for holding onto grudges, or resentment toward any group of peoples. We must also forgive any group, or culture that we believe have caused us, or anyone, harm and misfortune.

Forgiveness is instantly provided through grace, but even learning how to allow grace to move through us requires trusting higher ideals based in Love. Let go and let God.

Today, we begin releasing belief patterns than hinder us from being able to forgive other groups of peoples as a whole. In this practice, we pray for ourselves and all political world leaders. May trust become the foundation of future relationships between all nations.

Come to stillness, and then engage with the prayer below. Allow "space" for acceptance or tolerance to fill you as you contemplate the meaning of each sentence.

A PRAYER FOR FORGIVENESS

May we learn to accept each other, and forgive our grievances with one another. May we all become blessed with the power of forgiveness.

May we have the grace within to unconditionally forgive anyone who has done wrong toward us.

May we all have the strength to let go of thoughts of ill-will toward others.

May I have the strength to forgive my own past actions, and may I have the courage to trust others.

May our world leaders gain the strength and courage to offer forgiveness to all leaders of all nations, and may trust be established among all leaders of all nations.

May all of us learn how to release our anger, fear, and uncertainty within, so we may come to trust each other. May we now embrace our diverse world of peoples open heartedly.

May we learn to listen not only to hear, but to understand each other.

May we learn to accept our differences, prosper through them, and offer only kindness toward each other.

May we learn how to love each other, and take care of each of other.

                                                                    ~ Om

"If we cannot end now our differences, at least we can help make the world safe for diversity."

~ John F. Kennedy

Commencement Address at American University, June 10, 1963

Today we explore our capacity for the practice of tolerance.

This practice brings a powerful inner reward. Learning to offer tolerance for all beings will shift you into a condition of authentic joy. As you learn to accept all people for who they are, there is no longer a need to "build walls of protection" between you and any other person.

You remain in a constant state of calm so eventually; practicing tolerance is no longer any effort on your part. Instead, having tolerance for all beings becomes who you are. You and compassion become one.

Tolerance becomes a gift of freedom that you are able to offer others. The gift of acceptance, love, and understanding flows from you, giving both you and others the freedom to be who they are in that moment. May you become this joy.

OPEN HEART AND JOY MEDITATION

Come into a comfortable sitting or reclined position.

Close your eyes and allow stillness to occur. Focus on observing your inhale and exhale for 5 full breath cycles.

While focused on your breathing, expand your hearing wide.

Imagine your ears to be like satellite dishes that can hear all sounds in the world. Allow yourself to hear the laughter and giggling of children playing. Breathe, focus, and allow your mind's eye to create this scene.

As this vision forms in the mind's eye, allow yourself to "see" the faces of children from different cultures laughing and playing together. Allow this visualization to offer you a full experience of hearing. Settle the mind so that you hear and see the playing, the laughter, the sound of the breeze, or the sound of cars going by.

Allow yourself to now see the faces of the parents of these children. See them looking upon their children playing. See the parents smiling at their children. Look deep, and see the love flowing from their eyes toward their children.

Now, in your Heart Center, allow yourself to FEEL the joy these parents from other cultures are experiencing as they watch their children play. <u>Allow their joy to also be your joy</u>.

Expand this. Allow yourself to really FEEL it.

Imagine a cord of light connecting your heart with the hearts of the parents. Imagine cords of light connecting you with the children as well. All of you are connected as One.

Feel the connection. Feel the warmth of the laughter. Feel the peace of tolerance and acceptance.

Feel the unity of all peoples expressed through pure love.

When you are ready, you may end today's practice.

"If civilization is to survive, we must cultivate the science of human relationships – the ability of all peoples, of all kinds, to live together, in the same world at peace."

~ Franklin D. Roosevelt

Again, today we focus on the joy and peace that is found by practicing tolerance for the diversity among all peoples and cultures.

I invite you to purposefully seek out and befriend people outside of your current circle of friendships. Step out of your comfort zone, and speak to someone you normally would not.

Reach out and say, "Hello!" Smile, and let the light in your eyes shine through.

This practice involves *mindfulness in action* as we learn to notice others who would have normally escaped our attention.

In mindfulness, we now learn to see the potentiality of friendships, and *unity* in all the faces of diversity.

Explore diverse social classes; try new events or social gatherings that normally you would never attend. Go there, and say, "Hello." Expand your circle.

MINDFULNESS IN ACTION

Mindfulness is practicing awareness in each present moment. When we are fully aware, we allow each moment to be what it is, with no judgment.

Anytime we encounter a stranger, we have an opportunity to choose our intention in that moment. Remember however, the present moment can only be recognized through awareness of it.

Today, I invite you to see all strangers as "familiar friends." Smile at everyone you meet. Say hello to everyone.

If this feels uncomfortable to you at first, then try simply saying **"Namaste"** to yourself as you encounter each person.

Namaste' is a Sanskrit word, pronounced as NAH-məs-tay. It is a very powerful word, which roughly translates to mean:

"The Light in me honors the Light in you."

or

"The Spirit that lives through me honors the Spirit in you."

This single word, Namaste', when expressed inside of mindfulness, has the power to bridge the gap between all peoples. It removes perceived barriers, and allows peace to open all hearts.

May you learn to see the Light in all people.

~ **Om**

"Compassion is the signature of Higher Consciousness. Non-violence is the tool to evolve into Higher Consciousness."

~ Amit Ray

From: *Nonviolence: The Transforming Power* (2012)

Gandhi called the "power" that allows one to adhere to non-violent practices in effort to transform one's state of consciousness **Satyagraha**, which means "adherence to truth." The practice involves a willingness to modify one's belief patterns while a compassionate mindset develops over time.

Once compassion always becomes your choice, you will remain seated in Satyagraha. There will be no need to use harsh words, no desire to seek revenge, nor the wish to dominate anyone or any situation. Truth is the highest power, and can only be discovered inside the steady practice of compassion.

Living compassionately is a lifestyle not limited to those who are religious, follow any particular faith, or are of spiritual nature. This powerful state of consciousness is available to anyone brave enough to adhere to discovering the true nature of all things.

TRUTH AS A POWER

Truth is not the same as facts. Truth has power, whereas facts only provide information.

Truth is a force of power that is abundantly found inside a peaceful and calm mind.   This state of consciousness provides clarity, and an inward state of honesty that sets good intentions with power and confidence.

Therefore, the power of truth makes reconciliation and forgiveness possible.

Truth opens the heart and liberates us from any fear, hatred, or greed that would normally engage us in violent thoughts or actions.

MANTRA PRACTICE

Come into a comfortable sitting or reclined position. Close your eyes and allow stillness to occur.

Focus on observing your inhale and exhale for 5 full breath cycles.

Engage in today's mantra:

"May all choose the power of Truth."

"May all choose non-violence as Truth."

Stay with this repetition as long as you can.

If your mind becomes bored, then guide yourself into a visual meditation, allowing your mind's eye to send the power of Truth as an "idea" to any place of conflict in the world.

Breathe in Peace, and exhale Truth to the area or region in conflict.   Allow yourself to become a vessel of Truth. Allow breath to carry the intention of Truth for you.

"God of peace, bring your peace to
our violent world: peace in the
hearts of all men and women and peace
among the nations of the Earth."

~ Pope Benedict XVI

Bliss and happiness must first be discovered within before
these qualities can radiate from you.

As you continue with your peace meditations, you will notice
that as you more frequently cultivate inner peace through
stillness, prayer, and mantra, the more this "presence of peace"
stays with you, even during your busy moments each day.

We must use our freewill to choose this peace. We must
become aware of our inner peace within, and awaken it. We
must invoke it, engage with it, honor it, and allow it to work
through us.

The quote above is for all of us. May we each come to know
this peace, so our actions come from authentic peace.

ALLOWING THE PEACE WITHIN TO BE KNOWN

Come into a comfortable sitting or reclined position.

Close your eyes and allow stillness to occur. Focus on
observing your inhale and exhale for 5 full breath cycles.

Bring your mind's eye to one-pointed concentration, and focus on the space between your eyebrows. This physical location of your body is often referred to as the Third Eye.

Awareness of this place as a <u>portal of consciousness</u>, allows you the ability to directly experience your own source of inner wisdom.

Keep your attention at this point. Creating one-pointed, laser focused awareness of the mind's eye will cultivate a sense of inner peace automatically, once you have awakened it.

If, at this point in your practice you are unable to remain in focused concentration on the mind's eye, recite the prayer below to yourself 3 times after your meditation session:

PRAYER FOCUS IN PEACE

In the temple of my mind,
peace fills my mind, my body, and my heart.
Peace rises within, and peace radiates from my body.
Infinite peace fills me, surrounds me, and becomes me.

I accept this peace.

May all come into this peace.
May all families have wellness in this peace.
May peace come into the minds of all.
May peace take over every nation.
May peace prevail through the entire world.

~ Amen

"Dear God, please send to me
the spirit of Your peace.
Then send, dear Lord, the spirit
of peace from me to all the world."

~ Marianne Williamson

The power of prayer brings authentic inner peace to those who seek such peace. As more and more people genuinely experience their own source of inner peace, a higher potentiality for peaceful actions among all peoples will occur.

We must continue to pray for peace, no matter what is happening in the world around us. As more and more people pray for peace, contemplate peace, and act with peaceful intentions, the more peace will become a bridge between all beings.

The "gap" of divisions between us will be one day be bridged through our devotion to prayer, meditation, and dedication to each other.

In today's practice, we contemplate the power of peace through prayer.

You may use this prayer, your own, or any of the additional prayers in this guidebook.

A Prayer For Peace Among all Peoples

O God, you are the source of life and peace.

We know it is you who turns our minds to thoughts of peace.

Hear our prayer for peace.

Your Love lifts the minds and hearts of all peoples.

Muslims, Christians, and Jews all celebrate you in their own unique traditions. May we honor each other's faith tradition.

May all peoples; families, friends, and even foes, learn to speak to each other in absolute love and kindness.

May all who have been estranged now join hands and hearts in friendship and devotion.

May all nations seek the way of peace together.

Strengthen our resolve to give witness to these truths by the way we live.

Give to us:
Understanding that allows peace to grow,
Mercy that offers compassion to all,
Forgiveness that overcomes all pain,
And empower us to live in your law of love.

~ Amen

"First keep peace with yourself, then you can also bring peace to others."

~ Thomas à Kempis

Today, we again take time to offer ourselves kindness, rest, and compassion. Some days we may need to seek inner peace for our own well-being. This is a simple reality of being human.

When you feel tired, it is okay to rest. When you need companionship of like-minded people, seek it. When you need solitude, allow time for it.

Devotion to your peace practice requires regular inward attention. Find comfort within first, always. Taking time for oneself is not selfish. Knowing when to take personal refuge requires wisdom.

In this practice, we engage in contemplative prayer for our own well-being.

DEVOTED TO PEACE

Today's practice will be done in mindfulness. Prepare yourself a cup of tea, or any warm beverage.

Now, sit with it. Allow yourself to fully experience the cup of tea.

Pick up the cup. Feel the warmth in your hands. Take time to notice the aroma. Sip the beverage and fully experience the warm liquid passing your lips and throat.

Try to keep your mind focused on only experiencing the tea. If your mind begins to wander, bring your attention back to one-pointed concentration. Focus on feeling the cup's warmth.

Allow the activities of the day to fade away. Allow yourself to be restored into a state of calmness. Sit with your tea for a full 5 minutes, and <u>do</u> nothing else.

When you are ready, begin to contemplate the prayer below. Allow yourself to FEEL each word as you read it.

THE PRAYER

May peace be my guide. When weary, may the practice of peace be the comfort I seek.

May peace teach me to seek peace in the hearts of all those around me.

In peace, may I always speak well of all peoples, even when they are not in my presence.

May I become a light for others.
May I always treat all beings with loving-kindness.

May I bring joy to hearts and minds.
May my eyes shine with peace.

When you finish the prayer, and your tea, be mindful that today's session is complete. Allow yourself to feel restored by your own sense of inner peace.

"Do not overrate what you have received, nor envy others. He who envies others does not obtain peace of mind."

~ The Buddha

Practicing peace requires a certain amount of humbleness.

It is easy to entertain ideas of well-being by choosing to believe that we are better than others, or by allowing pride in our possessions to provide a sense of worth, or feeling that material success is a foundation for inner peace. These are all false ideas.

For example, on the other side of pride is envy, which is a condition we will experience if we compare ourselves to others and what they may have. Holding onto these ideas are false judgments, and will only disturb one's inner peace.

Peace is found inside a humble heart that "sees" all people as equal. A mind focused in peace, see all things as one. A humble heart is also a grateful heart. Simplicity is key. May we all rise to the "best" that peace has to offer.

MEDITATIVE CONTEMPLATION

This text is from the Tao, and is a wonderful writing to reflect upon as a meditation.

Allow yourself to come into stillness.   Allow the activities of the day to fade away.

Breathe.   Release all tension.   Free your mind to realize that in this present moment, all is well.   Find simplicity in this moment, and find gladness in it.   Guide your heart in this moment to become humble and grateful.

Cultivate in your heart, an all-knowing sense of peace. Now, focus on the text below, holding each word in your heart and fully FEEL the meaning of each word.

MEDITATION ON THE BEST PEACE

The Best

The best, like water,
benefit all and do not compete.
They dwell in lowly spots that everyone else scorns.
Putting others before themselves,
they find themselves in the foremost place
and come very near to the Tao.
In their dwelling, they love the earth;
in their heart, they love what is deep;
in personal relationships, they love kindness;
in their words, they love truth.
In the world, they love peace.
In personal affairs, they love what is right.
In action, they love choosing the right time.
It is because they do not compete with others
that they are beyond the reproach of the world.

Tao Te Ching, chapter 8.
Translation by Stephen Ruppenthal.

"I think it's naive to pray for world peace
if we're not going to change the form in
which we live."

~ Godfrey Reggio

As the quote suggests, it does no good to practice meditations
in peace, and then speak harshly to family, friends, co-workers,
the waitress, etc.

Nor, it is beneficial for anyone to engage in gossip, acts of
revenge, or to wish harm to any person or living thing.

Our prayers must be in alignment with our actions.   This is
cultivated by meditating and praying for the wisdom of peace
to fill you in all ways, but also through mindfulness in your
day-to-day living. In short, what you focus on expands.

Your meditation practice will become expressed outwardly as
daily positive actions, when you mindfully set your intention to
become *devoted* to peace in all that you say, and in all that you
do.

Additionally, by mindfully practicing peace each and every
day, and remaining committed to peace, peace does become
you. A calm mind becomes impossible to disturb.

Today, we mindfully contemplate this yogi's prayer.

Prayer for Peace

Adorable presence,
Thou who art within and without,
above and below and all around,

Thou who art interpenetrating
every cell of my being,

Thou who art the eye of my eyes,
the ear of my ears,
the heart of my heart,
the mind of my mind,
the breath of my breath,
the life of my life,
the soul of my soul,

Bless us, dear God, to be aware of thy presence now
and here.

May we all be aware of thy presence
in the East and the West,
in the North and the South.

May peace and goodwill abide among individuals,
communities, and nations.
This is my earnest prayer.

May peace be unto all!

Composed by Swami Omkar, the venerable head of Shanti
Ashram in Andhra Pradesh and of the Peace Center on the
Nilgiris, South India.

"Above all else, guard your heart, for everything you do flows from it."

~ Proverbs 4:23

Proverbs is a book of Wisdom found in the Old Testament, and this verse above is one of my favorite passages. Yes, we must guard our hearts, because in this *place* of feeling, we create our intentions.

This simple, yet profound wisdom text reminds us to guard the heart so we may remain aware of our truest intentions.

When the mind becomes turbulent, the heart follows with emotion. For this reason peaceful meditation practices are best experienced from either the mind's eye, or the Heart Center.

Remaining rooted in peace requires a calm mind, and a peaceful heart. May our intentions be born in peace and may our actions be good.

SETTING YOUR INTENTIONS IN PEACE

Come into a comfortable sitting or reclined position.

Close your eyes and allow stillness to occur.

Allow the activities of the day to fade away. Allow your mind to settle.

Bring your attention to the point between your eyebrows, the mind's eye.

With each inhale, bring more and more of your attention to this space. When random thoughts come into your awareness, let them pass with no judgment.

You may begin to see colors or shapes as you concentrate on this space. Allow those to pass.

When ready, FEEL yourself declare from your heart the intention below:

"May all my intentions be of Peace."

When ready, bring your attention to your Heart Center.

Allow your breath to expand Heart Center with each inhale. **With an expanded heart FEEL each word in this mantra:**

"My heart is kind."
"My heart is free to love and be loved."
"My heart is filled with the intention of peace always."

Try to focus on the mantra practice for 10-20 minutes.

When you are ready, you may end today's practice.

You will feel a sense of calm and peace throughout your entire body.

"Let there be work, bread, water and salt for all."

~ *Nelson Mandela*

Peace on Earth and goodwill towards all, equates with the realization that there is also abundance for all.

Peace on Earth negates oppression, poverty, and lack of any kind.

Peace on Earth celebrates diversity, and dances in gladness with every culture, and every living thing.

In our prayers for peace, we must also imagine peace entering into the minds and hearts of all so deeply, that every person and every living being will be afforded plentitude and wellness.

Peace on Earth is a principle that goes beyond non-violent action. Peace is more than non-killing.

Peace invokes goodwill towards all, which means that all beings are allowed equal opportunities for happiness, health, and prosperity.

In today's practice, we contemplate the words in this beautiful prayer written by Maya Angelou.

A Simple Prayer - Maya Angelou

Father, Mother, God,

thank you for your presence

during the hard and mean days.

For then we have you to lean upon.

Thank you for your presence

during the bright and sunny days,

for then we can share that which we have

with those who have less.

And thank you for your presence

during the Holy Days, for then we are able

to celebrate you and our families and our friends.

For those who have no voice, we ask you to speak.

For those who feel unworthy, we ask you to pour your love out

in waterfalls of tenderness.

For those who live in pain, we ask you to bathe them

in the river of your healing.

For those who are lonely,

we ask you to keep them company.

For those who are depressed, we ask you to shower upon them

the light of hope.

Dear Creator, You, the borderless sea of substance, we ask you

to give to all the world that which we need most—Peace.

ADDITIONAL PRAYERS

This section is provided for the days you wish to expand your meditation time during your daily practices. I have collected these prayers together from a variety of peoples, cultures and traditions. Each one provides insight and grace for the practice of peace.

May peace fill you and guide you.

A PRAYER FOR THE WORLD
by Rabbi Harold Kushner

Let the rain come and wash away
the ancient grudges, the bitter hatreds
held and nurtured over generations.
Let the rain wash away the memory
of the hurt, the neglect.
Then let the sun come out and
fill the sky with rainbows.
Let the warmth of the sun heal us
wherever we are broken.
Let it burn away the fog so that
we can see each other clearly.
So that we can see beyond labels,
beyond accents, gender, or skin color.
Let the warmth and brightness
of the sun melt our selfishness.
So that we can share the joys and
feel the sorrows of our neighbors.
And let the light of the sun
be so strong that we will see all
people as our neighbors.
Let the earth, nourished by rain,
bring forth flowers
to surround us with beauty.
And let the mountains teach our hearts
to reach upward to heaven.

~ Amen

WAGE PEACE
by Judyth Hill

*Wage peace with your breath. Breathe in firemen and rubble,
breathe out whole buildings and flocks of red wing blackbirds.*

*Breathe in terrorists and breathe out sleeping children
and freshly mown fields. Breathe in confusion and breathe
out maple trees.*

*Breathe in the fallen and breathe out lifelong friendships
intact. Wage peace with your listening: hearing sirens, pray
loud.*

*Remember your tools: flower seeds, clothes pins,
clean rivers.*

*Make soup. Play music, memorize the words for thank you in
three languages. Learn to knit, and make a hat.*

*Think of chaos as dancing raspberries, imagine grief as the
outbreath of beauty or the gesture of fish.*

Swim for the other side. Wage peace.

*Never has the world seemed so fresh and precious:
Have a cup of tea and rejoice.*

Act as if armistice has already arrived.

Celebrate today.

Matthew 5:3-10

Blessed are the poor in spirit:
for theirs is the kingdom of heaven.

Blessed are they that mourn:
for they shall be comforted.

Blessed are the meek:
for they shall inherit the earth.

Blessed are they which do hunger
and thirst after righteousness:
for they shall be filled.

Blessed are the merciful:
for they shall obtain mercy.

Blessed are the pure in heart:
for they shall see God.

Blessed are the peacemakers:
for they shall be called the children of God.

Blessed are they which are persecuted for righteousness' sake:
for theirs is the kingdom of heaven.

~ In thy Name of Peace

PRAYER FOR PEACE
By Pir-O-Murshid Inayat Khan

Send Thy peace O Lord, which is
perfect and everlasting,
that our souls may radiate peace.

Send Thy peace O Lord, that we
may think, act and speak harmoniously.

Send Thy peace O Lord, that we
may be contented and thankful for
Thy bountiful gifts.

Send Thy peace O Lord, that amidst
our worldly strife, we may enjoy Thy bliss.

Send Thy peace O Lord, that we
may endure all, tolerate all, in the thought of
Thy grace and mercy.

Send Thy peace O Lord, that our lives
may become a Divine vision and in Thy light,
darkness may vanish.

Send Thy peace O Lord, our Father and Mother, that we Thy
children on Earth may all unite in one family.

~ Amen

ABOUT THE AUTHOR

Melinda Johnston, M.Msc. Spiritual Philosopher and Coach, Intuitive Healer, Wellness Consultant, International Author and Speaker, Peace Activist

Melinda has over 25 years of study and practice in religious culture, practical philosophical, metaphysical sciences and understanding for the historical "webs" of human history, which have impacted most of our modern religions and today's current spiritual practices in Western society.

She is well versed in multiple facets of religious and sacred philosophy, including the Eastern philosophies of Buddhism and Vedanta, metaphysical consciousness, and the Yoga Sciences. Her gentle teaching method guides her students into obtaining the exact inner wisdom for expanding into deeper levels of awareness and well-being.

She believes practicing peace allows for profound transformations of consciousness to occur within.

"Peace meditation is simple, kind, nurturing, and Absolute. As peace develops within each individual person, it begins to radiate outward to become a powerful, healing force. May we all cultivate this Peace."

She has created a variety of alternative methods for celebrating life and seeing the "sacred" in simplicity.

As founder of The Buddhi Institute, her goal is to teach practical meditation methods, and spiritually based programs that incorporate mindfulness, yoga philosophy, and other ancient wisdoms, for the integration of mind and spirit.

"Mindfulness is meditation in action. Inspired action comes from a calm mind, and peaceful heart. Awareness within a higher state of consciousness allows complete peace and wellness to arise effortlessly into one's day-to-day living."

ABOUT BUDDHI INSTITUTE

Located in Rochester, NY, the Buddhi Institute offers a vast array of opportunities to deepen your well-being and spiritual practice. The programs and practices train you how to cultivate your own inner guidance.

The offerings from the Buddhi Institute empower students and clients with mindfulness training, consciousness studies, spiritual development, wellness retreats, and mastering the mind through practices belonging to the Yoga Sciences.

Offerings include:

1-to-1 Private Sessions
Guided Mastery Programs
Group Classes
Online Studies and Practices
Global Events
Spiritual and Wellness Retreats

FOR MORE INFORMATION GO TO:
www.buddhiinstitute.com

Your heart is the size of an ocean. Go find yourself in its hidden depths.

~ Rumi

95

ABOUT BUDDHI PRESS

B uddhi Press produces the workbooks, guidebooks, and teachings, which are used in both private coaching, group classes, and personalized Mastery Programs. Some of these materials are available for independent study.

The workbooks offer easy-to-learn spiritual practices to incorporate into your daily living. The suggestions for daily practice do not require hours and hours of reading. Most of the exercises or applications only take 2-20 minutes a day of dedication.

The practices do not require journaling, writing, or watching video after video. Those are Rational Mind activities. Buddhi Institute practices move you inward to experience consciousness beyond the limitations of Rational Mind. You are introduced to an idea, or a philosophical concept, which is explained thoroughly, so you may incorporate the practice into your day-to-day living.

These methods of practice give you actual experience in Quantum Laws, Ancient Philosophies, Yoga Wisdoms, and Spiritual Insights so you come to know how to experience your own personal innate Wisdom.

The goal of these practices is to obtain one-pointed centeredness, and mindfulness for the inner workings of the mind. As your inner awareness becomes known, you find yourself easily placed on a path of peace and that is in harmony with all aspects of your life.

At the time of printing this book, the following courses of study are obtainable through the online store:

Inspired Action
Seeing with the Heart
Chakras as Consciousness
Becoming a Quantum Activist
Listening to your Inner Wisdom
Introduction into Meditation and Mindfulness

BUDDHI PRESS
500 Helendale, Suite 260
Rochester, NY 14609
585-672-5250
insight@buddhiinstitute.com   www.buddhiinstitute.com

"Each one has to find his peace from within. And peace to be real must be unaffected by outside circumstances.

Non-violence is not a garment to be put on and off at will. Its seat is in the heart, and it must be an inseparable part of our being."

~ Gandhi

48627556R00056

Made in the USA
Middletown, DE
24 September 2017